HOLIDAY GREETINGS

I0884844

Decorate your home
for the holidays!

2

5

18

21

LEISURE ARTS, INC. • Maumelle, Arkansas

HAPPY EASTER

WITH ITS BRIGHTLY DECORATED EGGS, cute chick, fuzzy bunny, and pretty flowers, this adorable design is sure to add a pop of color to your home this Easter.

HAPPY EASTER (PART A)
120 × 81 threads

COLOR KEY

Note: Please read all instructions on page 24 before beginning.

Plastic Canvas Size Needed: 20" × 14"

Symbol	Color	Symbol	Color	Symbol	Color
■	Black	⬭	Light Blue	·	White
↑	Dark Blue	♡	Light Gray	★	Yellow
✳	Dark Purple	◣	Light Pink		**Backstitch Floss (4 strands)**
V	Gold	/	Lime Green	———	Black
●	Green	–	Orange	———	Rose
○	Lavender	✕	Rose		

Overcast the edges using White yarn.

Note: Please read all instructions on page 24 before beginning.

HAPPY EASTER (PART B)
120 × 81 threads

Gray area indicates last row of previous section of design.

COLOR KEY

■	Black
🡅	Dark Blue
✳	Dark Purple
V	Gold
●	Green
◑	Lavender
⬯	Light Blue
♡	Light Gray
◣	Light Pink
/	Lime Green
–	Orange
×	Rose
▪	White
★	Yellow

Backstitch Floss (4 strands)

———	Black
———	Rose

Overcast the edges using White yarn.

CHART LAYOUT

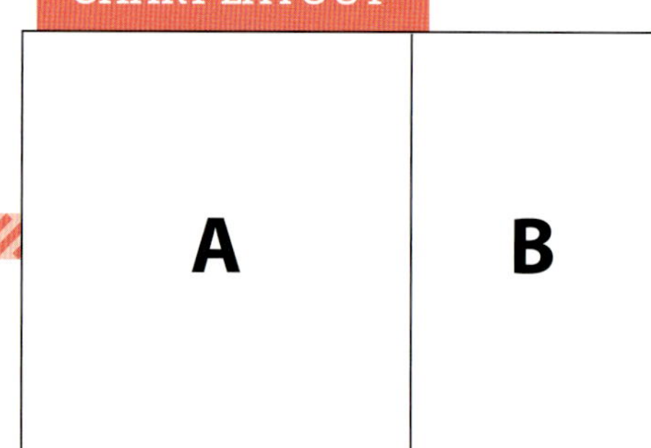

TRICK OR TREAT

NO TRICKS HERE—only this adorable treat to hang on your wall! This enchanting Halloween design will delight all the trick-or-treaters who visit your home.

T (#1)
31 × 36 threads

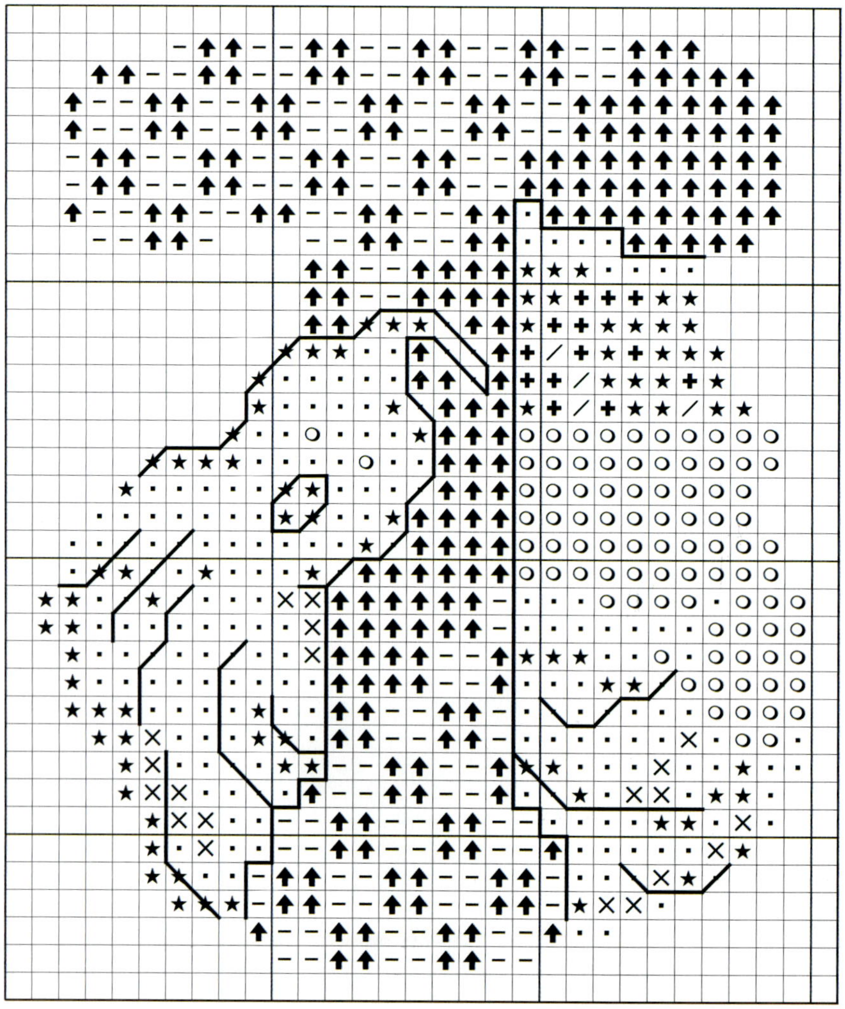

Note: Please read all instructions on page 24 before beginning.

COLOR KEY

○	Black
✚	Gold
⬆	Green
×	Light Blue
–	Lime Green
/	Orange
·	White
★	Yellow

Backstitch Floss (4 strands)

———	Black

Overcast the edges using yarn that matches the adjacent stitches.

R (#1)
30 × 38 threads

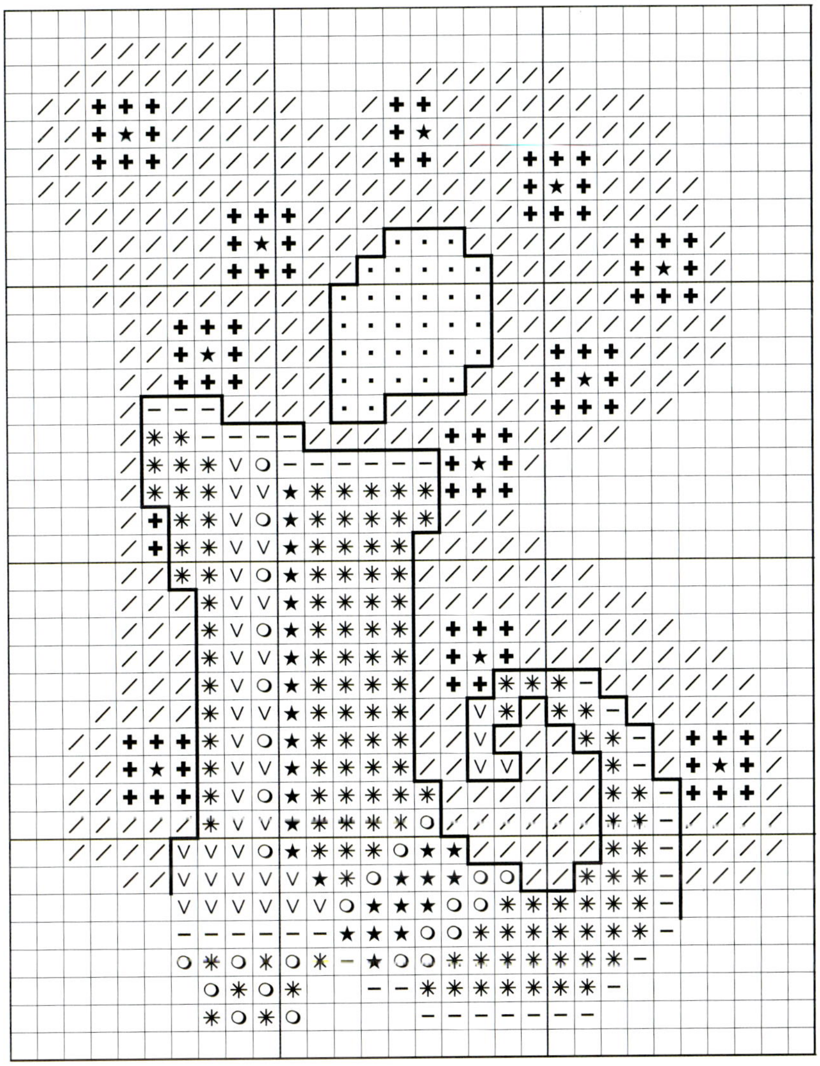

Note: Please read all instructions on page 24 before beginning.

COLOR KEY

○	Black
✳	Dark Blue
✚	Gold
V	Lavender
–	Lime Green
⁄	Orange
·	White
★	Yellow

Backstitch Floss (4 strands)

▬	Black

Overcast the edges using yarn that matches the adjacent stitches.

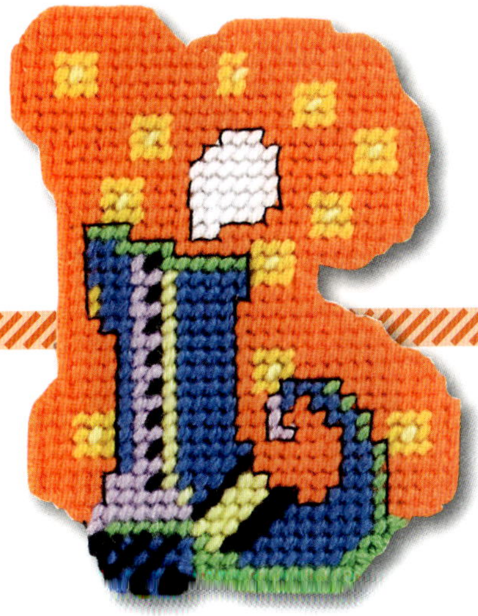

I
25 × 38 threads

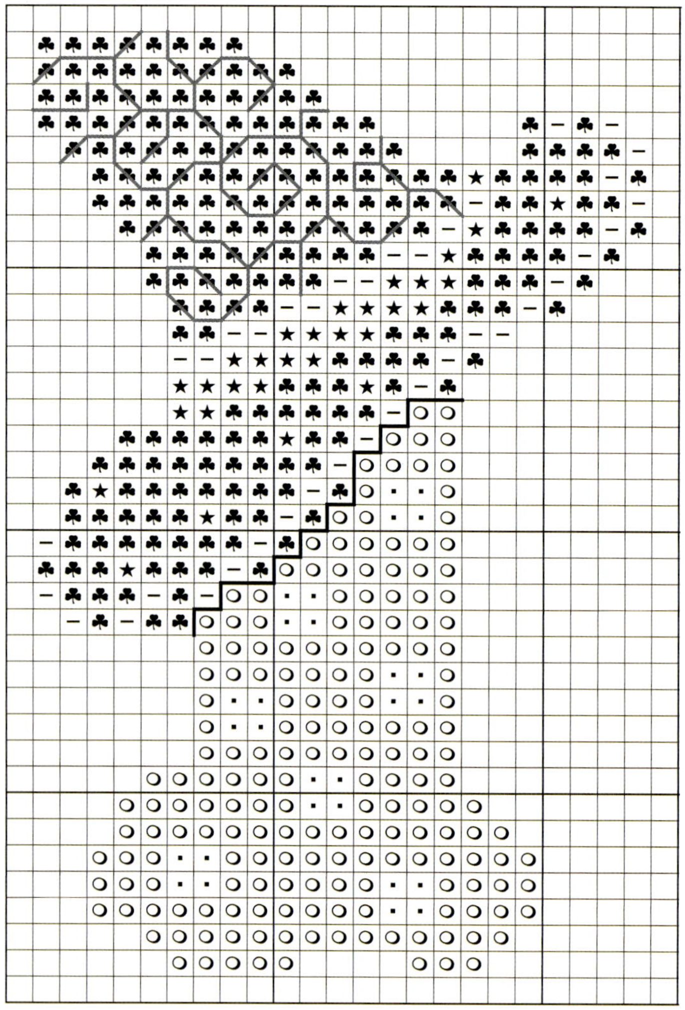

Note: Please read all instructions on page 24 before beginning.

COLOR KEY

❍	Black
♣	Dark Purple
–	Lime Green
▪	White
★	Yellow

Backstitch Floss (4 strands)

——— (black line)	Black
——— (gray line)	Yellow

Overcast the edges using yarn that matches the adjacent stitches.

C
32 × 35 threads

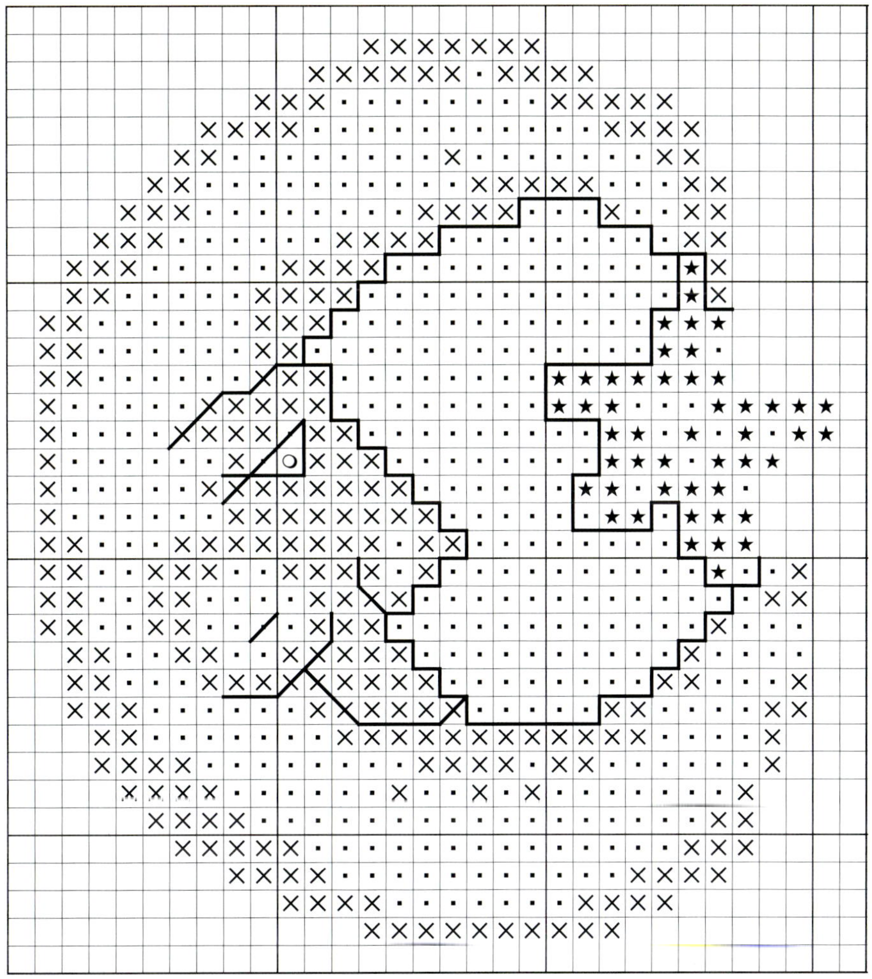

Note: Please read all instructions on page 24 before beginning.

COLOR KEY

Symbol	Color
❍	Black
×	Light Blue
·	White
★	Yellow

Backstitch Floss (4 strands)

Symbol	Color
———	Black

Overcast the edges using yarn that matches the adjacent stitches.

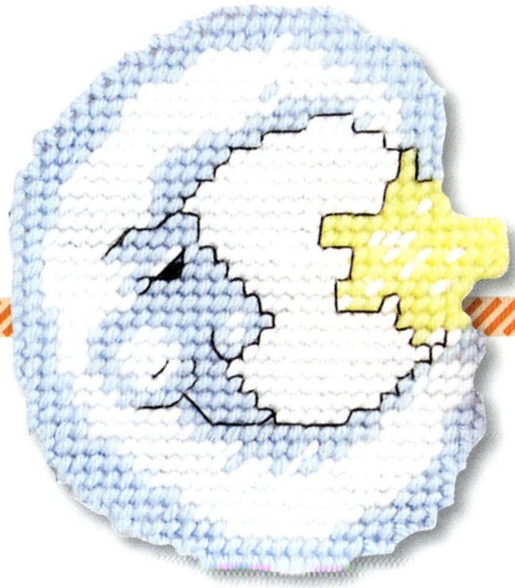

K
33 × 33 threads

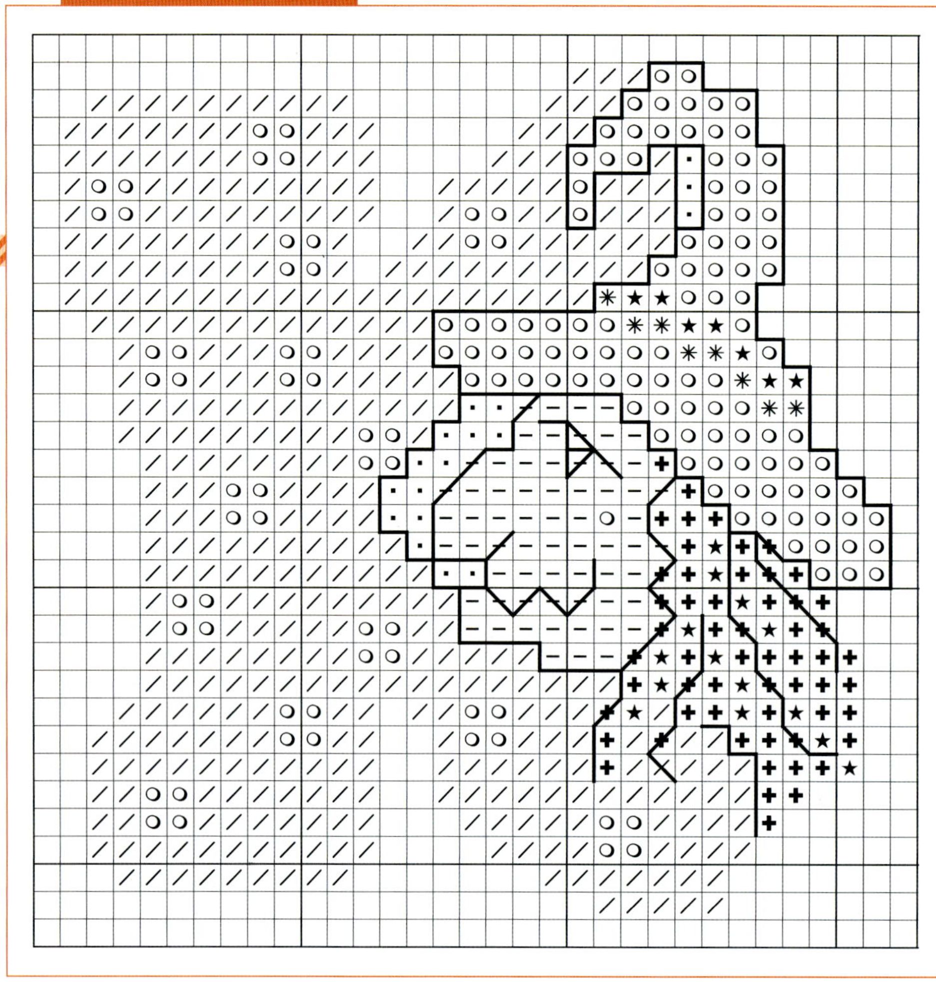

Note: Please read all instructions on page 24 before beginning.

COLOR KEY

❍	Black
✳	Dark Blue
✚	Gold
–	Lime Green
⁄	Orange
▪	White
★	Yellow

Backstitch Floss (4 strands)

——	Black

Overcast the edges using yarn that matches the adjacent stitches.

T (#2)
32 × 33 threads

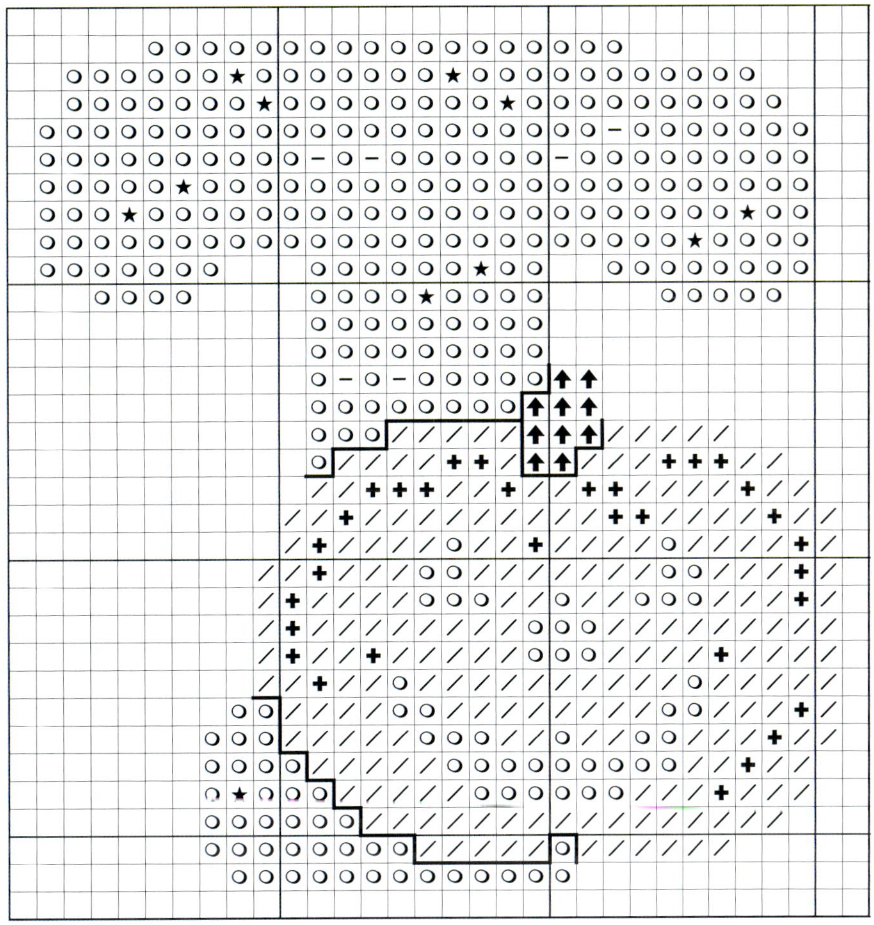

Note: Please read all instructions on page 24 before beginning.

COLOR KEY

❍	Black
✚	Gold
↑	Green
–	Lime Green
/	Orange
★	Yellow

<u>Backstitch Floss (4 strands)</u>

——	Black

Overcast the edges using yarn that matches the adjacent stitches.

R (#2)
28 × 32 threads

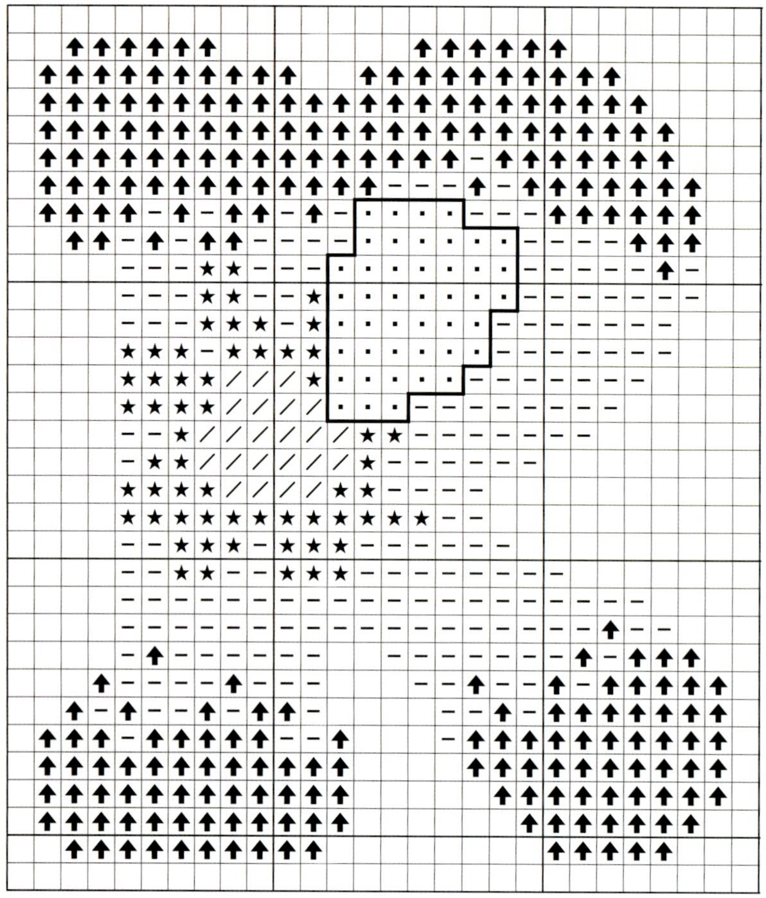

Note: Please read all instructions on page 24 before beginning.

COLOR KEY

🡅	Green
–	Lime Green
⁄	Orange
▪	White
★	Yellow

Backstitch Floss (4 strands)

——	Black

Overcast the edges using yarn that matches the adjacent stitches.

E
27 × 39 threads

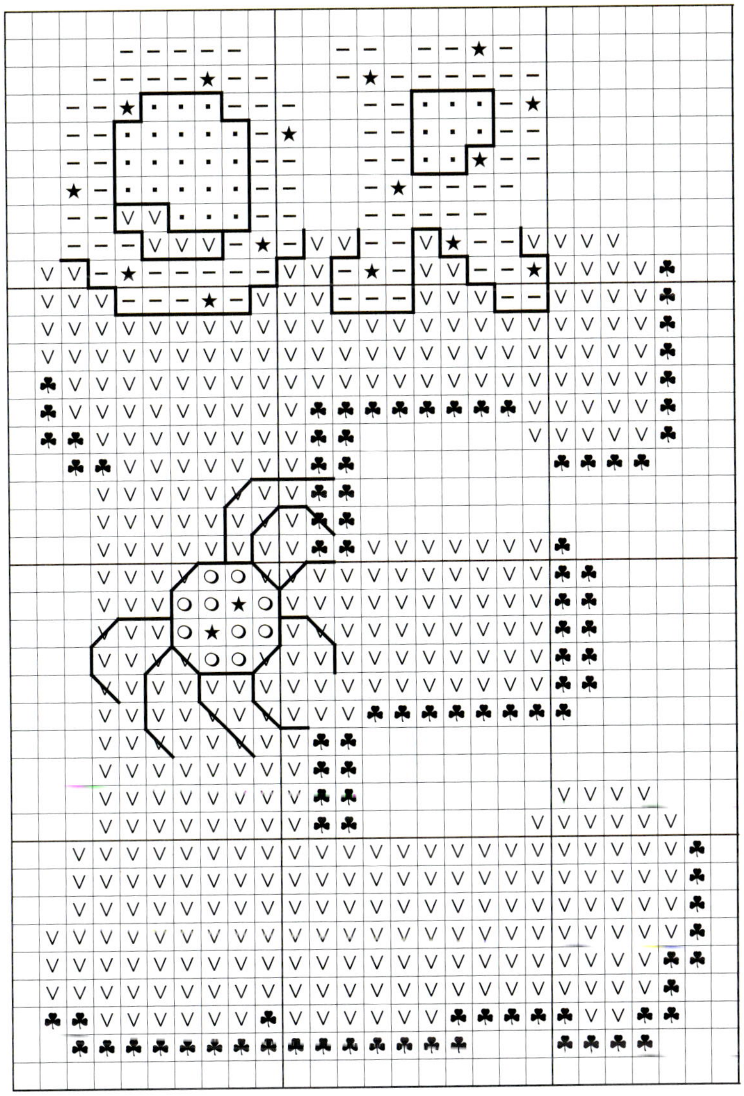

Note: Please read all instructions on page 24 before beginning.

COLOR KEY

Symbol	Color
❍	Black
♣	Dark Purple
V	Lavender
–	Lime Green
▪	White
★	Yellow

Backstitch Floss (4 strands)

Symbol	Color
———	Black

Overcast the edges using yarn that matches the adjacent stitches.

A
28 × 37 threads

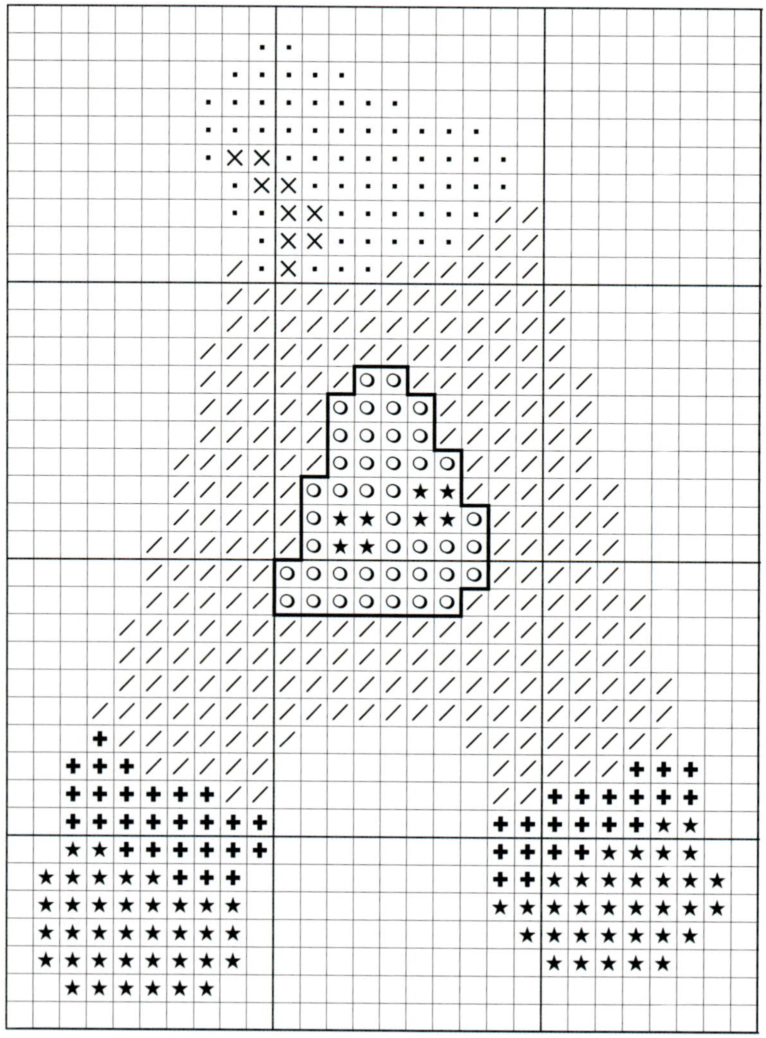

Note: Please read all instructions on page 24 before beginning.

COLOR KEY

❍	Black
✚	Gold
×	Light Blue
⁄	Orange
·	White
★	Yellow

Backstitch Floss (4 strands)

——— Black

Overcast the edges using yarn that matches the adjacent stitches.

T (#3)
32 × 36 threads

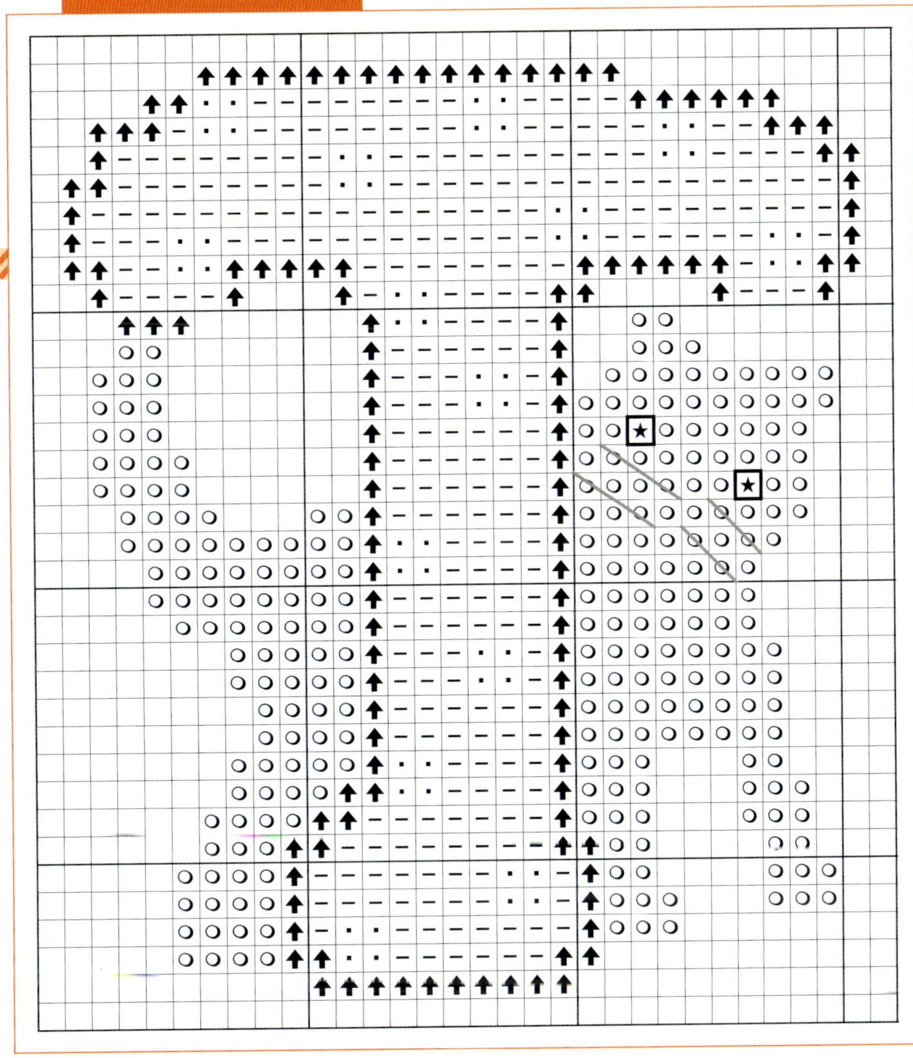

Note: Please read all instructions on page 24 before beginning.

COLOR KEY

○	Black
↑	Green
–	Lime Green
·	White
★	Yellow

Backstitch Floss (4 strands)

black line	Black
gray line	Yellow

Overcast the edges using yarn that matches the adjacent stitches.

Note: Please read all instructions on page 24 before beginning.

COLOR KEY

/	Orange
·	White

Backstitch Floss (4 strands)

——	Black

Overcast the edges using Orange yarn.

Finishing Instructions
After the letters have been stitched, cut out each letter and overcast the edges using yarn that matches the adjacent stitches. Overcast the edges of the web using Orange yarn. Glue felt backing to the back of each letter and the web. Referring to the photo for placement, glue the letters in place on the web.

CHART LAYOUT

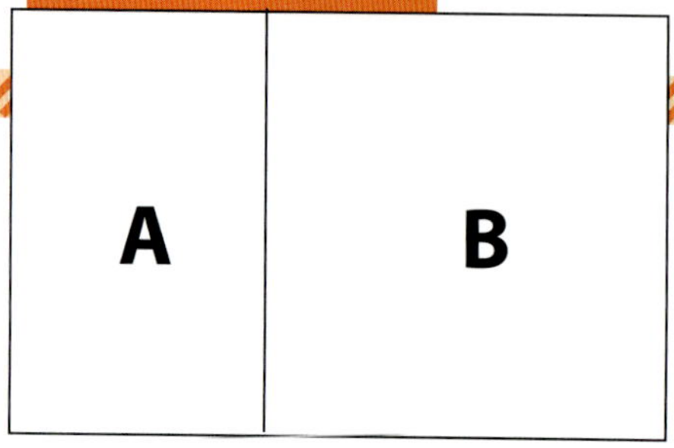

WEB (PART A)
128 × 86 threads

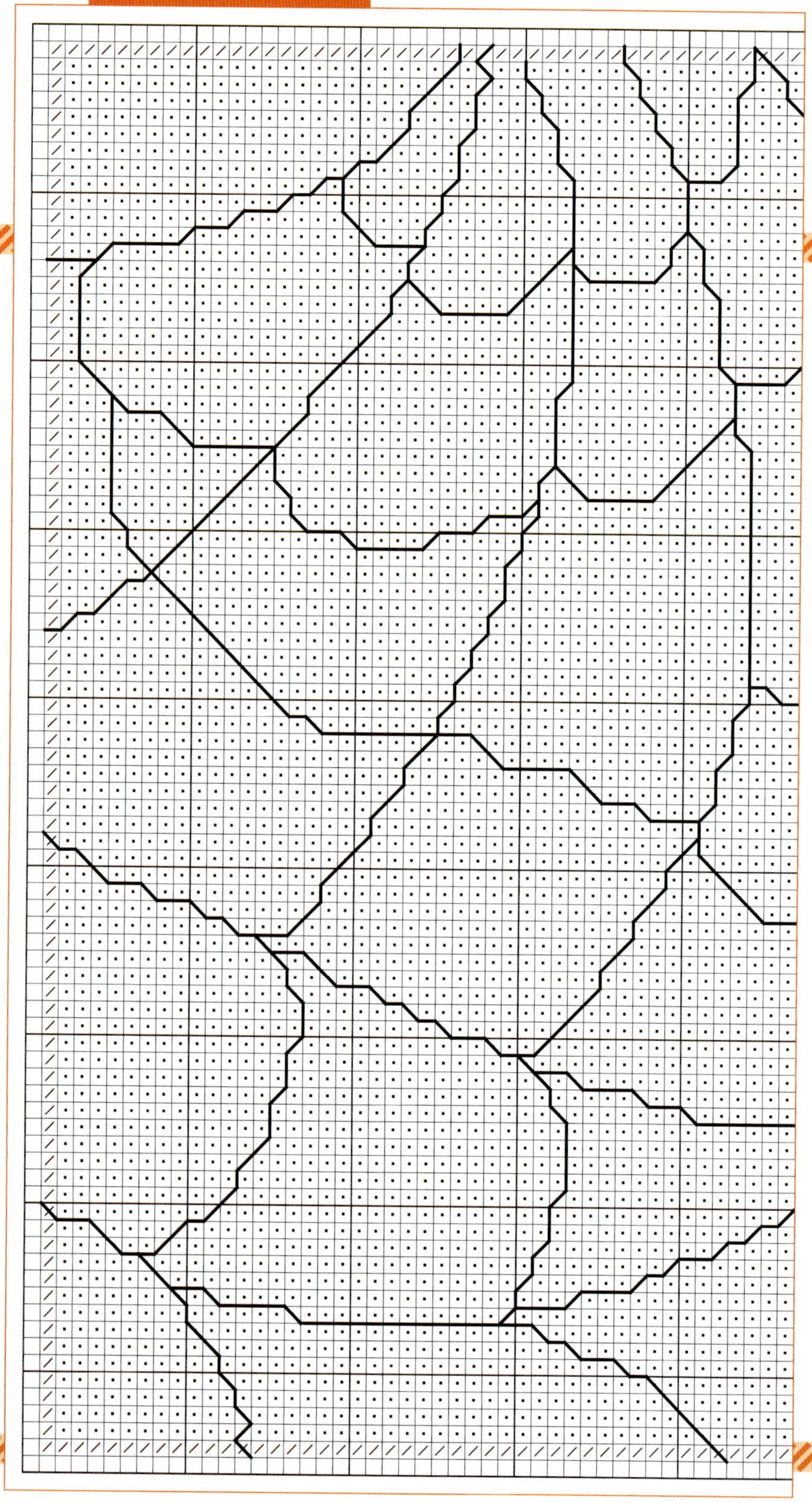

Plastic Canvas Size Needed: 21" × 15"

WEB (PART B)
128 × 86 threads

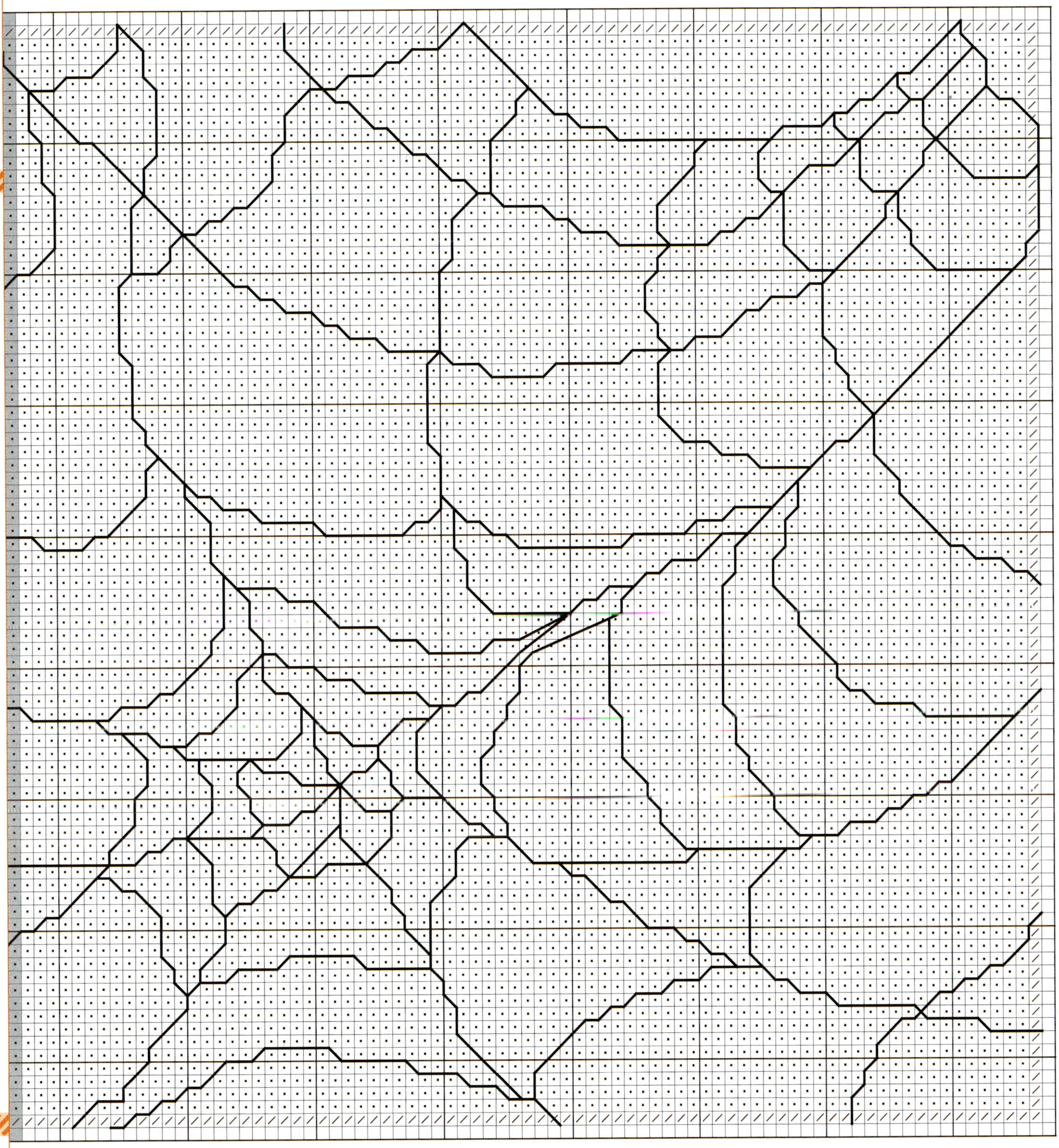

Gray area indicates last row of previous section of design.

GIVE THANKS

CHARMING WOODLAND CRITTERS and harvest motifs decorate this delightful autumn design. Whether displaying it just during Thanksgiving or choosing to showcase it all throughout fall, it's sure to bring a little warmth to your home.

Note: Please read all instructions on page 24 before beginning.

COLOR KEY

- ■ Black
- / Cream
- ✿ Dark Brown
- – Dark Green
- ^ Gold
- ○ Gray
- ★ Light Brown
- ◣ Light Gray
- ⧗ Light Yellow
- ◇ Lime Green
- ✳ Orange
- ⬆ Red
- × Sage
- ● Tan
- · White
- ꞩ Yellow

Backstitch Floss (4 strands)

- Black
- Dark Brown
- Dark Green

Backstitch Floss (4 strands)

- Light Brown
- Light Yellow
- Orange

Algerian Eyelet Floss (4 strands)

- Light Yellow
- Lime Green
- Orange

Overcast the edges using cream.

GIVE THANKS (PART A)
119 × 81 threads

Plastic Canvas Size Needed: 20" × 14"

COLOR KEY

■	Black
/	Cream
✿	Dark Brown
–	Dark Green
^	Gold
○	Gray
★	Light Brown
◣	Light Gray
⧗	Light Yellow
◇	Lime Green
✳	Orange
⬆	Red
×	Sage
●	Tan
▪	White
S	Yellow

Backstitch Floss (4 strands)

- Black
- Dark Brown
- Dark Green

Backstitch Floss (4 strands)

- Light Brown
- Light Yellow
- Orange

Algerian Eyelet Floss (4 strands)

- Light Yellow
- Lime Green
- Orange

Overcast the edges using yarn that matches the adjacent stitches.

GIVE THANKS (PART B)
119 × 81 threads

Note: Please read all instructions on page 24 before beginning.

Gray area indicates last row of previous section of design.

CHART LAYOUT

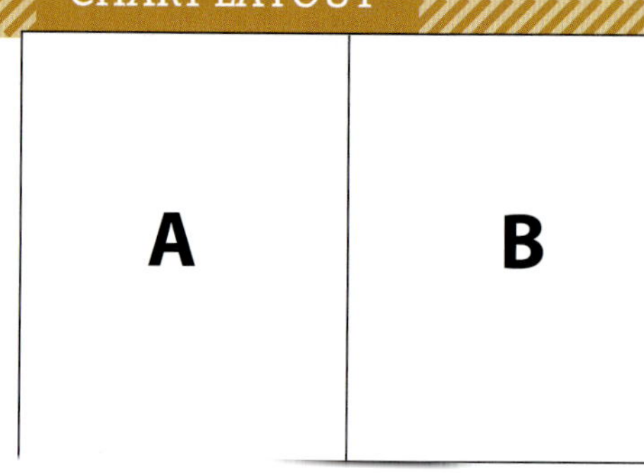

MERRY CHRISTMAS

GET IN THE HOLIDAY SPIRIT while stitching this festive design, which features all our favorite things about Christmas—from gifts and stockings to ornaments and jingle bells!

Note: Please read all instructions on page 24 before beginning.

COLOR KEY

■	Black
✳	Dark Blue
⬆	Dark Green
●	Dark Red
$	Gold
+	Green
–	Lavender
∟	Light Blue
☽	Light Pink
△	Lime Green
◇	Red
▪	White
◣	Yellow

Backstitch Floss (4 strands)

———	Black
〰	Red

Backstitch Metallic Floss (6 strands)

———	Antique Gold
- - - -	Royal Blue

Overcast the edges using yarn that matches the adjacent stitches.

MERRY CHRISTMAS (PART A)

118 × 80 threads

Plastic Canvas Size Needed: 18" × 14"

CHART LAYOUT

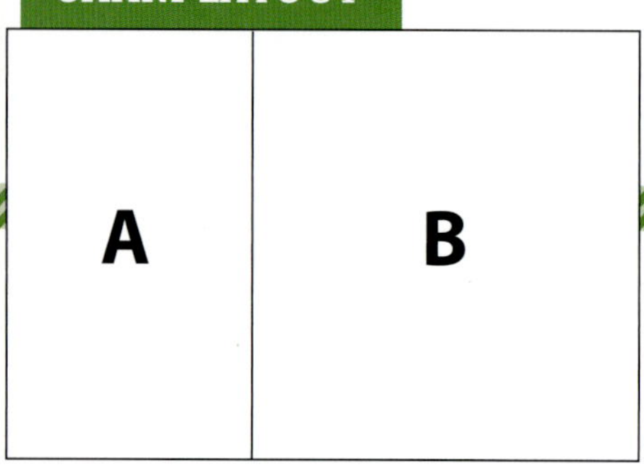

MERRY CHRISTMAS (PART B)
118 × 80 threads

Gray area indicates last row of previous section of design.

GENERAL INSTRUCTIONS

QUICK TIPS

1. Prior to beginning a project, look over the requirements and directions carefully.
2. Stitch the design on an uncut piece of plastic canvas to avoid snagging yarn or floss on ragged edges. If necessary, cover the edge with masking tape to avoid snags.
3. Some designs require a piece of plastic canvas larger than the standard 10½" x 13½" size. Consult the larger designs for the size of plastic canvas needed and stitch on a piece that accommodates the design size (the smaller designs will fit on a standard sheet of plastic canvas). The designs can also be stitched on two smaller pieces of plastic canvas that equal the required size when joined. Start stitching the top of the design at the top of the first piece of plastic canvas. When you get to the bottom of the first piece, line up the second piece of plastic canvas and use a half cross stitch to continue the next row in the design (see diagram). As you stitch, make sure the holes in both pieces of plastic canvas line up correctly.

4. For a finished look, trim rough edges and cut off corners at an angle.
5. All pieces are stitched on 7-mesh plastic canvas using a size 16 tapestry needle and worsted weight yarn. Floss details use 4 strands of cotton embroidery floss or 6 strands of metallic floss.

STARTING TO STITCH

All stitches begin on the back of your work. With a threaded needle, come up from the back of your work, hold a 1" section of the yarn against the back of the canvas and stitch over the 1" section. This will eliminate the need for a knot on the end of your yarn and will keep the back side of your work clean and flat. To finish off a color, run the needle under 4 or 5 stitches on the back and clip off. The tension of the stitches will hold the yarn in place and knots will not be necessary.

DIRECTIONS

- Stitch the piece(s). Except where otherwise indicated, ½ cross stitch is used for all main areas.
- To work the charts, start with the top left stitch using the yarn color indicated on the chart and color key. Bring the needle up from the back of the work at the symbol indicated to create the first stitch (see diagram).
- Cut away surplus canvas. Cut outside and trim the rough edges next to unworked edges. Overcast all edges.

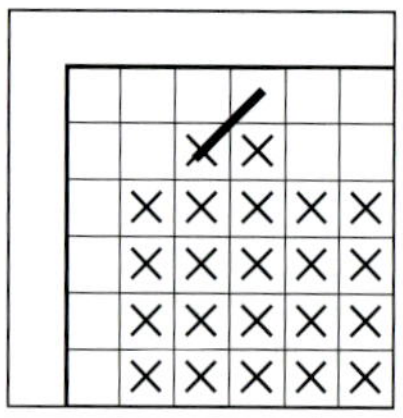

CUTTING YOUR CANVAS

Always cut your canvas between the bars, making sure to leave one plastic bar between the stitches and cutting line. By cutting between the bars, you will be assured an adequate amount of plastic for overcasting the edges when finishing (see diagram).

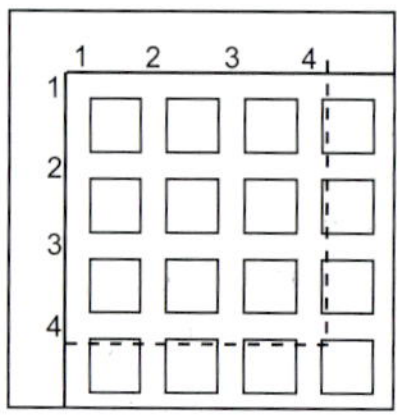

CLEANING

Hand-wash plastic canvas projects in warm water with a mild soap. Do not rub or scrub stitches, as this will cause the yarn to fuzz. Do not put your stitched piece in the dryer; allow to air dry.

STITCH GUIDE

½ Cross Stitch

Most commonly used, it is either stitched in rows or columns. This stitch slants up from left to right. Always bring the needle up on odd numbers and down on even numbers.

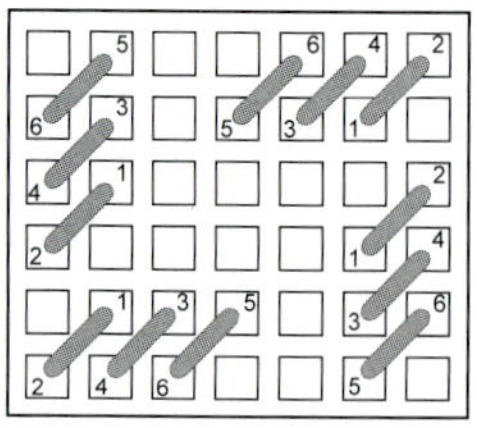

Overcast Stitch

This stitch is used for finishing your edges or joining two pieces of canvas. The stitch comes up in one hole, over the border bar and up the next hole, over the border bar and up the next hole.

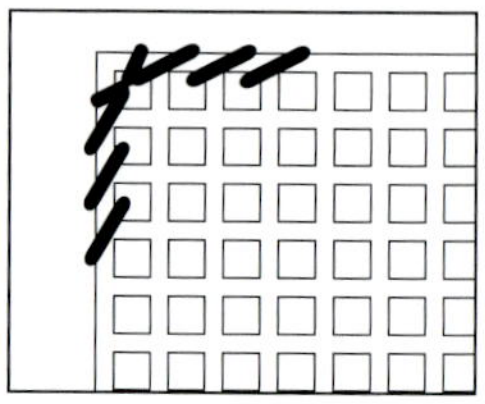

Backstitch

A backstitch is made in any direction with multiple continuous stitches crossing one bar at a time.

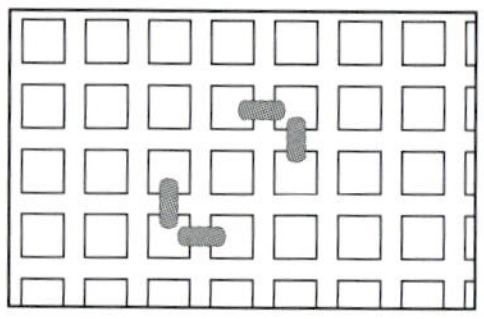

Algerian Eyelet

Bring the threaded needle up through the canvas at the top center of the stitch. Go over one bar of canvas and down through the center hole. Come up at the upper right corner of the stitch, and down through the center hole. Work clockwise in this manner to complete the eyelet.

Produced by Herrschners, Inc., for distribution exclusively by Leisure Arts, Inc., 104 Champs Blvd., STE 100, Maumelle, AR 72113-6738, leisurearts.com.